Peace, Be Still

A 31-Day Christmas Prayer Journal

For to us a child is born, to us a son is given;
and the government shall be upon his shoulder, and his name shall be called
Wonderful Counselor, Mighty God, Everlasting Father, Prince of Peace.
— Isaiah 9:6

Peace, Be Still: A 31-Day Christmas Prayer Journal
by Courtney Joseph

Join the Community

WomenLivingWell.org

GoodMorningGirls.org

Facebook.com/WomenLivingwell

Facebook.com/GoodMorningGirlsWLW

Instagram.com/WomenLivingWell

#WomenLivingWell

#PeaceBeStill

Table of Contents

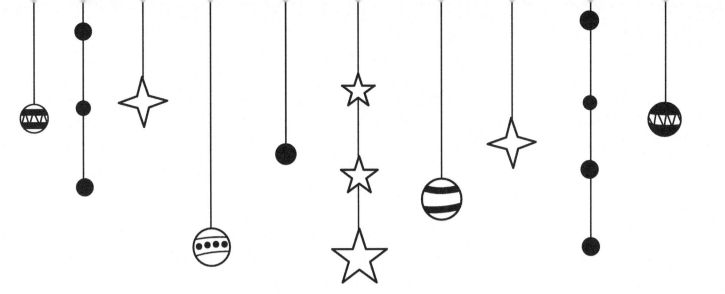

Introduction

"When they saw the star they were overjoyed.
On coming to the house, they saw the child with his mother Mary
and they bowed down and worshiped him."
— MATTHEW 2:10

Every year, our family piles into the car to drive around looking at Christmas lights. Before we leave the house, I have the children color a few pictures of baby Jesus. Then I write a little note on the picture and have the kid's sign it. As we drive by the houses, we look for nativity scenes. We have to search hard because nativities are not a frequent sight. But when we find one —oh the excitement! The kids clap and cheer as they anticipate putting their picture in the newspaper box with the note that says, *"Thank you for displaying the reason for the season – Jesus."*

But on the night that Jesus was born, there were no loud claps and cheers. He was born in a humble stable. In a humble stable, God became flesh.

"The Word became flesh and made his dwelling among us.
We have seen his glory, the glory of the One and Only."
— JOHN 1:14

Think about the word "flesh". When we accidentally cut ourselves, it's our flesh that bleeds. God became flesh.

"Immanuel – God with us."
— MATTHEW 1:23

This is the real meaning of Christmas. It's not about the holiday ham and cookies, or Christmas lights and decorations, or Santa and reindeer, or baby dolls and Legos! It's about Jesus - coming in the flesh. God dwelt among us. And he went from the stable to the cross because of his love for you and me.

You are so very loved. So, let's take the time to stop, be still and linger at the feet of Jesus, each day in the month of December, by being in his word and prayer.

Peace. Be Still.

Jesus is with you and he is the Wonderful Counselor, the Mighty God, the Everlasting Father and the Prince of Peace.

For to us a child is born, to us a son is given;
and the government shall be upon his shoulder and
*his name shall be called **Wonderful Counselor, Mighty God,***
Everlasting Father, Prince of Peace.
— ISAIAH 6:9

Have a very Merry Christmas.

Keep walking with the King of Kings!

Courtney
WomenLivingWell.org, GoodMorningGirls.org

Wonderful Counselor

The Hope of Christmas

Jesus' Birth Foretold
LUKE 1:26-37

In the sixth month the angel Gabriel was sent from God to a city of Galilee named Nazareth, [27] to a virgin betrothed to a man whose name was Joseph, of the house of David. And the virgin's name was Mary. [28] And he came to her and said, "Greetings, O favored one, the Lord is with you!" [29] But she was greatly troubled at the saying, and tried to discern what sort of greeting this might be. [30] And the angel said to her, "Do not be afraid, Mary, for you have found favor with God. [31] And behold, you will conceive in your womb and bear a son, and you shall call his name Jesus. [32] He will be great and will be called the Son of the Most High. And the Lord God will give to him the throne of his father David, [33] and he will reign over the house of Jacob forever, and of his kingdom there will be no end."

[34] And Mary said to the angel, "How will this be, since I am a virgin?"

[35] And the angel answered her, "The Holy Spirit will come upon you, and the power of the Most High will overshadow you; therefore, the child to be born will be called holy—the Son of God. [36] And behold, your relative Elizabeth in her old age has also conceived a son, and this is the sixth month with her who was called barren. [37] For nothing will be impossible with God."

When the Spirit of truth comes, he will guide you into all the truth, for he will not speak on his own authority, but whatever he hears he will speak, and he will declare to you the things that are to come.

JOHN 16:13

DAY 1

Reflection

Jesus came as the savior of the world! This sweet baby born in a manger, died for you and me. For those who believe, he has given us the Holy Spirit as a guarantee of our salvation and Isaiah 9:6 says, Jesus is the "Wonderful Counselor." He is wonderful because He is both God and man. His counsel comes straight from the throne room of heaven and he guides us into truth.

In what area of your life are you in need of guidance or counsel? Write it out below and then be still and wait on the Lord, to show you his way.

_____

_____

_____

_____

_____

_____

_____

Dear God,

_____

_____

_____

_____

_____

_____

All Scripture is breathed out by God and profitable for teaching, for reproof, for correction, and for training in righteousness, that the man of God may be competent, equipped for every good work.

2 TIMOTHY 3:16-17

DAY 2

Reflection

Have you ever had a friend, who when you go to them with a problem, they simply get it. They understand you and they can perceive what is best in your situation? We need to remember that this little baby, born in a Bethlehem stable, is not just a warm fuzzy story for our children, but he is our Wonderful Counselor! Jesus understands you, when no one else does. Jesus is there for you, when you are all alone. Right now as you sit and read this, he is with you and he knows your every thought and your innermost hurts and needs.

How does this comfort you to know that you are never alone and he is always with you?

_____

_____

_____

_____

_____

_____

_____

_____

_____

Dear God,

_____

_____

_____

_____

_____

_____

_____

And the angel answered her, "The Holy Spirit will come upon you, and the power of the Most High will overshadow you; therefore, the child to be born will be called holy – the Son of God.

LUKE 1:35

DAY 3

Reflection

This child born in Bethlehem, the Saviour of the world, is ours! He exceeds all expectations. He fulfills all his promises. He is the reason for all our to-do lists, decorating, shopping and baking. He is our cause for rejoicing. As our calendars begin to fill up, may we not lose sight of this.

Take a moment now to pause and reflect on what Jesus has done for you. List below three or more things he has done and then give him praise.

_____

_____

_____

_____

_____

_____

_____

_____

_____

_____

Dear God,

_____

_____

_____

_____

_____

_____

_____

For no prophecy was ever produced by the will of man, but men spoke from God as they were carried along by the Holy Spirit.

2 PETER 1:21

DAY 4
Reflection

God is always speaking; all we have to do is start listening. God speaks to us primarily through his word. His word is truth. We need to be in his word! But sometimes he guides us through open and closed doors or he guides us through godly counselors and godly friends. Sometimes he guides us during times of worship, in our thoughts through the Holy Spirit. Do you need more guidance from the Lord?

Seek him today through one of the ways listed above – get into his word, talk to a godly friend, listen to an online sermon or spend time in worship. Reflect on your daily life. In what ways do you need to work on listening to God more?

_____

_____

_____

_____

_____

_____

_____

_____

Dear God,

_____

_____

_____

_____

_____

_____

_____

I will instruct you and teach you
in the way you should go;
I will counsel you
with my eye upon you.

PSALM 32:8

DAY 5

Reflection

You are never alone. God's eyes are always on you. He wants to instruct you and teach you in the way you should go. He wants to be our wonderful counselor but how often do we find ourselves talking over a problem with a friend for an hour, instead of reading scripture for an hour. It just seems easier to talk to a friend but if we will allow God to be our ultimate counselor, in 10 years we will be in an entirely different place than if we hadn't.

Write your favorite scripture passage below. God is speaking to you through that passage right now. Write out what he is saying to you and how it applies in this season of life.

_____

_____

_____

_____

_____

_____

_____

_____

Dear God,

_____

_____

_____

_____

_____

_____

_____

And your ears shall hear a word behind you,
saying, "This is the way, walk in it,"
when you turn to the right or
when you turn to the left.

ISAIAH 30:21

DAY 6

Reflection

Sometimes when it seems that God is not speaking, we need to take a step out in faith. Take one step in the direction that you feel he may be leading you, and then wait on God to give you further direction. At times, I have done this only to find that I was way off track and was getting ahead of God. Other times, I have taken a step out in faith and have found I was right in the center of God's will. Ultimately, what God wants from us is for us to yield to his lead.

In what ways are you yielding to God's lead in your life today?

_____

_____

_____

_____

_____

_____

_____

_____

_____

Dear God,

_____

_____

_____

_____

_____

_____

Have I not commanded you?
Be strong and courageous.
Do not be frightened,
and do not be dismayed,
for the Lord your God
is with you wherever you go.

JOSHUA 1:9

Reflection

Are you worried about something today? Thoughts that are filled with worry and anxiety do not come from God. He wants us to be strong and courageous and to know that he is always with us, no matter where we go. To combat worry – read God's word, meditate on God's word, memorize God's word, pray God's word and stand on the promises of God's word. He is our wonderful counselor and being in the word, helps us know the voice of God, so we can detect when a thought does not match the voice of God.

What thoughts are you having today, that do not come from God and how can you exchange your worry for strength and courage?

_____

_____

_____

_____

_____

_____

_____

Dear God,

_____

_____

_____

_____

_____

_____

_____

Mighty God

God With Us

The Birth of Immanuel

MATTHEW 1:18-25

Now the birth of Jesus Christ took place in this way. When his mother Mary had been betrothed to Joseph, before they came together, she was found to be with child from the Holy Spirit. ¹⁹ And her husband Joseph, being a just man and unwilling to put her to shame, resolved to divorce her quietly. ²⁰ But as he considered these things, behold, an angel of the Lord appeared to him in a dream, saying, "Joseph, son of David, do not fear to take Mary as your wife, for that which is conceived in her is from the Holy Spirit. ²¹ She will bear a son, and you shall call his name Jesus, for he will save his people from their sins." ²² All this took place to fulfill what the Lord had spoken by the prophet:

²³ "Behold, the virgin shall conceive and bear a son, and they shall call his name Immanuel" (which means, God with us). ²⁴ When Joseph woke from sleep, he did as the angel of the Lord commanded him: he took his wife, ²⁵ but knew her not until she had given birth to a son. And he called his name Jesus.

LUKE 2:1-7

In those days a decree went out from Caesar Augustus that all the world should be registered. ² This was the first registration when Quirinius was governor of Syria. ³ And all went to be registered, each to his own town. ⁴ And Joseph also went up from Galilee, from the town of Nazareth, to Judea, to the city of David, which is called Bethlehem, because he was of the house and lineage of David, ⁵ to be registered with Mary, his betrothed, who was with child.

⁶ And while they were there, the time came for her to give birth. ⁷ And she gave birth to her firstborn son and wrapped him in swaddling clothes and laid him in a manger, because there was no place for them in the inn.

He is the radiance of the glory of God and the exact imprint of his nature, and he upholds the universe by the word of his power. After making purification for sins, he sat down at the right hand of the Majesty on high.

HEBREWS 1:3

DAY 8

Reflection

Isaiah 9:6 tells us that one of Jesus' names is "Mighty God". Jesus is the King of Kings! He is robed in majesty. He is strong, mighty and supreme over all creation. He has all authority, all sovereignty, all power, and all dominion. He is magnificent, beautiful, supreme in his splendor and none compares to Him. Oh, that we would grasp how awesome our God really is! Then we would not doubt. Then we would fully trust in Him. Then he would be our strength. Then we would love and adore him as he deserves.

How have you seen the power of Jesus revealed in your life?

_____

_____

_____

_____

_____

_____

_____

_____

_____

Dear God,

_____

_____

_____

_____

_____

_____

_____

And the Word became flesh and dwelt among us,
and we have seen his glory,
glory as of the only Son from the Father,
full of grace and truth.

JOHN 1:14

DAY 9

Reflection

When we come before the Lord, we come before a glorious and powerful God. When we worship him, all we are doing is recognizing the splendor that he already has. Many times, our worship is nowhere near what he is due. We can spend more time preparing our outer appearance for Sunday morning worship — than our hearts. He is worthy of more than just our Sunday morning worship for an hour or two. Worship should be our way of life.

Do you spend more time on your outer self than your inner? In what ways do you seek to glorify God in your daily life?

_____

_____

_____

_____

_____

_____

_____

_____

_____

Dear God,

_____

_____

_____

_____

_____

_____

_____

The Lord your God is in your midst,
a mighty one who will save;
he will rejoice over you with gladness;
he will quiet you by his love;
he will exult over you with loud singing.

ZEPHANIAH 3:17

DAY 10

Reflection

God IS love and his love for you has no end. Over and over we are told in scripture and shown in scripture that God loves us. Our doubts do not change God's love for us. His love is steadfast and constant. When you are God's child, no matter what you do good or bad – he still loves you.

Do you struggle with accepting and believing God's love for you? How does remembering the deep love of God for you, quiet your soul and give you peace?

_____

_____

_____

_____

_____

_____

_____

_____

_____

Dear God,

_____

_____

_____

_____

_____

_____

_____

But Jesus looked at them and said,
"With man this is impossible,
but with God all things are possible."

MATTHEW 19:26

DAY 11
Reflection

In difficult times, I have asked God to intervene, and in that moment, it has not felt like God intervened. But who knows what he has protected me from? Perhaps things could have been ten times worse than they were and I will never know it. God has protected me and brought me through every trial I have ever faced. He is faithful! Are you facing the impossible? Or maybe struggling with anxiety about something that feels impossible? That roadblock in front of you may not disappear with one prayer. But this I can assure you; God is not hiding from you and he does hear your prayers.

In what area do you need to trust God more?

_____

_____

_____

_____

_____

_____

_____

Dear God,

_____

_____

_____

_____

_____

_____

_____

Finally, be strong in the Lord
and in the strength of his might.

EPHESIANS 6:10

DAY 12

Reflection

Inner turmoil is real, even for strong believers. Sometimes we tell believers who are discouraged or who struggle with anxiety to just pray more, believe more, and have more faith. But I can testify that sometimes you can be doing all of that and still feel discouraged. It's part of living in a fallen world. Your story is not done yet. God is still at work in a thousand different ways, even when you cannot see it.

Are you discouraged about something in your life? Write about it below and then think back and remember all that God has already done in your life. Keep trusting in him. Our God is faithful.

_____

_____

_____

_____

_____

_____

_____

_____

Dear God,

_____

_____

_____

_____

_____

_____

_____

For we do not have a high priest who is unable to sympathize with our weaknesses, but one who in every respect has been tempted as we are, yet without sin.

HEBREWS 4:15

DAY 13

Reflection

We have a savior who understands our temptations and trials. He is able to sympathize with our weaknesses. In Mark 3:9, Jesus told his disciples to have a boat ready for Him because the crowd was crushing Him. Jesus had to have an escape. Friends, if we carry the weight of all the needs of those around us, we will be crushed. Sometimes we need to escape. I say this for all the women reading today, who are pouring themselves out for the needs of others and feeling overwhelmed. Remember, even Jesus got away and needed rest. It is okay to rest.

Did you need to hear that today? Is there an area in your life where you need to say no or get away, so you are not so overwhelmed? Write about it below and take it to the Lord in prayer. Then be strong and protect yourself from becoming overextended.

_____

_____

_____

_____

_____

_____

_____

Dear God,

_____

_____

_____

_____

_____

_____

_____

Fear not, for I am with you;
be not dismayed, for I am your God;
I will strengthen you, I will help you,
I will uphold you with my
righteous right hand.

ISAIAH 41:10

DAY 14

Reflection

If you are a perfectionist or a woman with high ideals, maybe you need to hear this today. Perfect women aren't real, and real women aren't perfect. Striving for perfection will hurt you and lead you astray. Know this, we are not left alone in our imperfections. We are all a work in progress. We must lean hard on God daily, to help us become the woman he created us to be. When we are discouraged, we must remember that the God of the universe says to us, "*I am with you. Do not be discouraged for I am your God; I will strengthen you and help you.*" That's our Mighty God! He is Immanuel – God with us. We need only to turn to him and allow him to help us.

In what area of your life do you need strength and help? Do not try to do it all on your own.

_____

_____

_____

_____

_____

_____

Dear God,

_____

_____

_____

_____

_____

_____

WEEK 3

Everlasting Father

Worship the King of Kings

The Visit of the Wise Men

MATTHEW 2:1-12

Now after Jesus was born in Bethlehem of Judea in the days of Herod the king, behold, wise men from the east came to Jerusalem, ² saying, "Where is he who has been born king of the Jews? For we saw his star when it rose and have come to worship him." ³ When Herod the king heard this, he was troubled, and all Jerusalem with him; ⁴ and assembling all the chief priests and scribes of the people, he inquired of them where the Christ was to be born. ⁵ They told him, "In Bethlehem of Judea, for so it is written by the prophet:

⁶ "'And you, O Bethlehem, in the land of Judah, are by no means least among the rulers of Judah; for from you shall come a ruler who will shepherd my people Israel.'"

⁷ Then Herod summoned the wise men secretly and ascertained from them what time the star had appeared. ⁸ And he sent them to Bethlehem, saying, "Go and search diligently for the child, and when you have found him, bring me word, that I too may come and worship him." ⁹ After listening to the king, they went on their way. And behold, the star that they had seen when it rose went before them until it came to rest over the place where the child was. ¹⁰ When they saw the star, they rejoiced exceedingly with great joy. ¹¹ And going into the house, they saw the child with Mary his mother, and they fell down and worshiped him. Then, opening their treasures, they offered him gifts, gold and frankincense and myrrh. ¹² And being warned in a dream not to return to Herod, they departed to their own country by another way.

For the wages of sin is death,
but the free gift of God is eternal life
in Christ Jesus our Lord.

ROMANS 6:23

DAY 15

Reflection

Isaiah 9:6 tells us that one of Jesus' names is "Everlasting Father". Our God is unchanging. His strength, might, majesty and holiness will last forever. He reigns eternally. This is our God. This is the King that we get to walk with daily! Jesus died on the cross for our sins. He is with us and he loves us. May we sing his praises forever!

Have you repented of your sins and placed your faith in Jesus and received the free gift of eternal life? If you haven't, do it now! If you have, you are a child of God and he is your everlasting father. How has he transformed your life?

_____
_____
_____
_____
_____
_____
_____
_____

Dear God,

_____
_____
_____
_____
_____
_____
_____

Before the mountains were brought forth,
or ever you had formed the earth and
the world, from everlasting to everlasting,
you are God.

PSALM 90:2

Reflection

God existed before the mountains. He is the one who created them. Ponder this for a moment -God is from everlasting to everlasting. He is from eternity past and he will exist forever, through eternity future. You are a child of the Wonderful Counselor, the Mighty God, and the Everlasting Father. He is ours forever and not even death can separate us from him. Actually, death will take us nearer to him.

Is it hard for your mind to comprehend how God can have no beginning and no end? How does knowing that you are a child of God – forever, comfort you?

_____

_____

_____

_____

_____

_____

_____

_____

Dear God,

_____

_____

_____

_____

_____

_____

"I am the Alpha and the Omega"
says the Lord God, "who is and who was
and who is to come, the Almighty."

REVELATION 1:8

DAY 17

Reflection

Alpha is the first letter of the ancient Greek alphabet and omega is the last letter. Jesus said, he is the alpha and omega. He was at the beginning and he will be at the end. He is the almighty one and he is in sovereign control over the past, present and future. But trusting God, when life hurts, can be difficult. We wonder why he lets bad things happen. I can't give you the answer to your why, but this I know...all of our suffering is meant to point us back to God. God knows our greatest need is him and when we have him, we can have peace in the midst of our trials.

Are you facing something difficult today? How can you trust him more, knowing that he is in control and he loves you?

_____

_____

_____

_____

_____

_____

_____

Dear God,

_____

_____

_____

_____

_____

_____

_____

Jesus Christ is the same
Yesterday and today
And forever.

HEBREWS 13:8

DAY 18
Reflection

One thing is certain in life – change. Change can be hard. The loss of a friendship, a job change, or a little weight gain that changes my size, causing me to have to buy new clothes, can be frustrating. Most of us like things to be predictable and familiar but that is not how this world works. All of our lives, things will continue to change but Jesus never changes. He is the same yesterday, today and forever. He is a secure anchor for our souls, in the midst of life's storms.

In what area of your life do you fear change? How does knowing that God's word, God's love and God's presence never changes, calm your fears?

_____

_____

_____

_____

_____

_____

_____

Dear God,

_____

_____

_____

_____

_____

_____

The LORD appeared to him from far away.
I have loved you with an everlasting love;
therefore I have continued my
faithfulness to you.

JEREMIAH 31:3

DAY 19
Reflection

Is there someone in your life who has betrayed or rejected you? God's love is permanent, unchanging and forever. He loves us with an everlasting love and will continue to be faithful to you. Through Christ, there is no rejection. Through Christ, there is no condemnation. Through Christ, there is no separation from God. Let your soul enter deeply into these truths and find rest and joy there.

Have you suffered the rejection of someone close to you? How does knowing that God loves you completely and will never leave you, bring healing and comfort to your heart today?

_____

_____

_____

_____

_____

_____

_____

_____

Dear God,

_____

_____

_____

_____

_____

_____

And this is eternal life, that they know you,
the only true God, and Jesus Christ
whom you have sent.

JOHN 17:3

DAY 20
Reflection

Eternal life comes through knowing Jesus. Your soul is eternal. It will go on and on and on. It has no end. And so eternal life is a gift for those who believe in Jesus' death and resurrection, for the forgiveness of their sins. The minute that you come into a right relationship with Jesus, you step into eternal life. You will now live forever as a child of God. Nothing can separate you from his love.

Write about the day or the season of life when you came to know Jesus personally and then thank him for the free gift of eternal life.

_____

_____

_____

_____

_____

_____

_____

_____

Dear God,

_____

_____

_____

_____

_____

_____

Have you not known?
Have you not heard?
The Lord is the everlasting God,
the Creator of the ends of the earth.
He does not faint or grow weary;
his understanding is unsearchable.

ISAIAH 40:28

DAY 21

Reflection

Are you feeling weary and worn out today? God never grows weary and so, God wants us to bring all of our worries and cares to him in prayer. Why? Because there is an enemy who wants to devour us. And when that enemy strikes, we will only be able to stand firm in God's strength. Since this week is a holiday week, it may be harder than most to squeeze time in for prayer. Finding time to pray is not going to be easy, but it is possible and worth fighting for!

So, pause right now and write below the things that are making you weary. Know that God understands. Trust God to give you the strength you need, for each day as you depend on him.

_____

_____

_____

_____

_____

_____

_____

_____

Dear God,

_____

_____

_____

_____

_____

_____

_____

WEEK 4

Prince
of Peace

Peace, Be Still

The Angels Rejoice
LUKE 2:8-21

And in the same region there were shepherds out in the field, keeping watch over their flock by night. [9] And an angel of the Lord appeared to them, and the glory of the Lord shone around them, and they were filled with great fear. [10] And the angel said to them, "Fear not, for behold, I bring you good news of great joy that will be for all the people. [11] For unto you is born this day in the city of David a Savior, who is Christ the Lord. [12] And this will be a sign for you: you will find a baby wrapped in swaddling clothes and lying in a manger." [13] And suddenly there was with the angel a multitude of the heavenly host praising God and saying,

[14] "Glory to God in the highest, and on earth peace among those with whom he is pleased!"

[15] When the angels went away from them into heaven, the shepherds said to one another, "Let us go over to Bethlehem and see this thing that has happened, which the Lord has made known to us." [16] And they went with haste and found Mary and Joseph, and the baby lying in a manger. [17] And when they saw it, they made known the saying that had been told them concerning this child. [18] And all who heard it wondered at what the shepherds told them. [19] But Mary treasured up all these things, pondering them in her heart. [20] And the shepherds returned, glorifying and praising God for all they had heard and seen, as it had been told them.

[21] And at the end of eight days, when he was circumcised, he was called Jesus, the name given by the angel before he was conceived in the womb.

Do not be anxious about anything, but in everything by prayer and supplication with thanksgiving let your requests be made known to God.
And the peace of God, which surpasses all understanding, will guard your hearts and your minds in Christ Jesus.

PHILIPPIANS 4:6-7

DAY 22

Reflection

Isaiah 9:6 tells us that Jesus is the "Prince of Peace". He does not want us to be worried about anything. No matter what you face and no matter how hard it gets, keep trusting in God. Also, he tells us to pray about everything. Everything means all things. No matter how big or how small it seems, if it is worrying you, pray about it. Our God is personal. He is listening and he cares.

What do you need to give over to God today? Exchange your worry for his peace and be still. Jesus loves you!

_____

_____

_____

_____

_____

_____

_____

_____

_____

_____

Dear God,

_____

_____

_____

_____

_____

_____

Now may the Lord of peace himself
give you peace at all times in every way.
The Lord be with you all.

2 THESSALONIANS 3:16

DAY 23

Reflection

During hard times, God does not always show up the way I want him to. Like a toddler stomping her feet, I want God to give me what I ask for, when I ask for it. Instead, God knows my deeper needs. He knows I need to completely focus on Him. He knows I need comfort. He knows I need increased faith. He knows I need to depend on Him alone. He knows I need changed and that I need more of Him. Our outside circumstances may not change when we cry out to God in prayer, but our inner self – our soul and spirit – is comforted and calmed by the Prince of Peace.

How has God comforted you with His peace during difficult times?

_____

_____

_____

_____

_____

_____

_____

Dear God,

_____

_____

_____

_____

_____

_____

_____

_____

And while they were there, the time came for her to give birth. And she gave birth to her firstborn son and wrapped him in swaddling clothes and laid him in a manger, because there was no place for them in the inn.

LUKE 2:6,7

DAY 24

Reflection

Christmas is simple...yet complex. The baby in the manger...simple. The baking cookies, decorating, shopping, attending parties and concerts and family get-togethers...complex. Look at today's passage in Luke 2:6-7. Where were the women? The town was clearly full of women because there was no room in the inn, yet no women were there at Jesus' birth. Perhaps they were simply too busy doing other good things to show up. But they missed it! They missed Immanuel – God with us – being born. Let's not be so busy we miss Jesus this Christmas.

Pause now and just be with Jesus. Give thanks to God for sending his son.

_____

_____

_____

_____

_____

_____

_____

_____

Dear God,

_____

_____

_____

_____

_____

_____

_____

For to us a child is born, to us a son is given; and the government shall be upon his shoulder, and his name shall be called Wonderful Counselor, Mighty God, Everlasting Father, Prince of Peace.

ISAIAH 9:6

DAY 25

Reflection

Jesus' birth fulfilled prophecy. He came as both fully God and fully man and his names describe who he is and what he came to do. He is a Wonderful Counselor. There is no one more qualified to guide your life than him. He is the Mighty God. He is the one worthy of all worship and praise. He is the Everlasting Father. He has no beginning and no end. He is the Prince of Peace. When we trust in him, he causes our hearts to be at peace.

What is stealing your peace today? Be still. Give it to Jesus and have a very Merry Christmas!

_____

_____

_____

_____

_____

_____

_____

_____

_____

Dear God,

_____

_____

_____

_____

_____

_____

And let the peace of Christ rule in your hearts,
to which indeed you were called in one body.
And be thankful.

COLOSSIANS 3:15

DAY 26

Reflection

Sometimes when we long for peace, we think it will come through one more workout, one more girls night out, one more vacation or one more dollar earned – but the workouts, nights out and vacations all come to an end. Money is spent and we are back on the hamster wheel of life, running towards nowhere. We are deceived by our eyes and the lies of the world. We try to control our lives rather than live a surrendered life to God. We must be shaped by the word, not by the world.

Do you feel like you are stuck on a hamster wheel? Is there something in your life that you need to surrender to God? Write about it below.

_____
_____
_____
_____
_____
_____
_____
_____

Dear God,

_____
_____
_____
_____
_____
_____

Peace I leave with you;
my peace I give to you.
Not as the world gives do I give to you.
Let not your hearts be troubled,
neither let them be afraid.

JOHN 14:27

DAY 27

Reflection

We google and click and scroll and click and listen to YouTube and podcasts, in search of answers. We buy book after book and watch movie after movie, to escape our troubles. We plan far off travels, to get away from it all, but our baggage inside our souls, goes with us. Don't get me wrong – God gave us many good things to enjoy, but if we are not careful, these things will become poor substitutes for intimacy with God. He is the only one that can give us true peace.

How do you try to escape troubles in your life? What are some healthier habits you can form so that God's peace will rule in your heart?

_____

_____

_____

_____

_____

_____

_____

_____

Dear God,

_____

_____

_____

_____

_____

_____

_____

Come to me, all who labor and are
heavy laden, and I will give you rest.
Take my yoke upon you, and learn from me,
for I am gentle and lowly in heart,
and you will find rest for your souls.

MATTHEW 11:28-29

DAY 28

Reflection

All of us have burdens. Like a student weighed down with her backpack – we each have our own backpack, filled with stuff. We must remember that we have a Heavenly Father who wants to carry our bags for us. When we get onto an airplane, we have the choice to check our baggage or carry it on. I hope today you will choose to check it – give it to Jesus – don't carry it any longer.

What is weighing you down today? What do you need to let go of?

_____

_____

_____

_____

_____

_____

_____

_____

Dear God,

_____

_____

_____

_____

_____

_____

_____

"I have said these things to you,
that in me you may have peace.
In the world you will have tribulation.
But take heart: I have overcome the world."

JOHN 16:33

Reflection

Jesus tells us that we will all face hard times, but he does not want us to get discouraged by them. Sometimes, when we face hard times, it's easy to get rattled and overly emotional. But we cannot follow God's will and live in his peace when we are dominated by our emotions. Our emotions will lead us astray, so it's an act of obedience to control ourselves and obey God, even when we don't feel like it. When you don't know what to do because your emotions have blinded you, pray and ask God to teach you His will. God wants to lead you into his peace, into his joy, into his love and onto level ground.

Do you trust that God has your best interests in mind even in the midst of hard times?

_____

_____

_____

_____

_____

_____

_____

_____

Dear God,

_____

_____

_____

_____

_____

_____

_____

The Lord bless you and keep you;
the Lord make his face to shine upon you
and be gracious to you;
the Lord lift up his countenance upon you
and give you peace.

NUMBERS 6:24-26

DAY 30

Reflection

Life has many twists and turns each day. It is very easy to become frazzled and frustrated. In our own strength, we cannot be peaceful and thankful. This is where Christ changes everything! While many things will happen in your home this week that feel out of your control, there is one constant...God. God is with you. He tells us that his face is shining upon us. How amazing!

What are some good things that God has done in your life this year? Give thanks to God for both the big and small blessings in your life.

_____

_____

_____

_____

_____

_____

_____

_____

Dear God,

_____

_____

_____

_____

_____

_____

May the Lord give strength to his people!
May the Lord bless his people with peace!

PSALM 29:11

DAY 31

Reflection

Today is a day of reflection. Let's look back at the past year and evaluate your walk with God and then look ahead to the new year and commit to going deeper in your relationship with him. The Lord gives his people strength and peace to face the storms of life that this world cannot give. The peace the world gives is gone the second we face conflict or a problem, but the peace God gives, the world cannot give to you nor take away from you. How awesome is that truth!

What are some things that got in the way of your walk with God this last year? What are some things you will do this coming year to strengthen your walk with God? Keep walking with the King of Kings!

_____

_____

_____

_____

_____

_____

_____

Dear God,

_____

_____

_____

_____

_____

_____

Peace, Be Still

For to us

a child is born, to us a son is given;
and the government shall be upon his shoulder,
and his name shall be called

Wonderful Counselor,
Mighty God,
Everlasting Father,
Prince of Peace.

— ISAIAH 9:6

Made in the USA
Columbia, SC
14 November 2020

24537262R00050